Are You There, God?

K A R E N ▼ D O C K R E Y

A leader's
Edition
is available
for use
in group study

VICTOR BOOKS

A DIVISION OF SCRIPTURE PRESS PUBLICATIONS INC.
USA CANADA ENGLAND

Other SonPower Small Group Studies
Can We Talk, God? (devotional life)
Can't Fight the Feelings (emotions)
Why Not Love All of Me? (whole-person relationships)
Where Do You Think Sex Came From? (sexuality)
What's a Kid Like Me Doing in a Family Like This? (family relationships)
Leading from the Back of the Line (servant leadership)
Are You There, God? (knowing God)

ISBN: 1-56476-089-8
Cover Design: Joe DeLeon

1 2 3 4 5 6 7 8 9 10 Printing/Year 97 96 95 94 93

Produced by the Livingstone Corporation. David R. Veerman and J. Michael Kendrick, project staff.

Printed in the United States of America.

CONTENTS

This study about the character of God starts with your questions. I'm convinced that when you ask questions and discover the answers to those questions, you understand God better. And as you understand God, you are better able to commit to and grow in Him. As you explore important questions such as "Is God there?" and "How can I know God's will?" you discover crucial aspects of the nature of God, namely, that God is there, that He wants a personal relationship with you, that He guides you through pain, that He cares about your daily needs, that He has already revealed most of His will in the Bible, and that the life He offers is better than any other option.

ABOUT THE AUTHOR

KAREN DOCKREY has worked with teens and their leaders for over 18 years. She served two churches as minister of youth and currently spends her professional time writing for youth and their leaders. Her 17 books include *The Youth Workers' Guide to Creative Bible Study* (Victor Books) and another Life Support Small Group study: *What's a Kid Like Me Doing in a Family Like This?* She earned a Master of Divinity degree from Southern Baptist Theological Seminary and currently works with youth at Bluegrass Baptist Church in Hendersonville, Tennessee.

▼

ONE

Are You
There, God?

 HEARTBEAT

Reveal Your Hidden Questions

Find and circle ten questions people ask about God. (Hint: the answers read diagonally as well as vertically and horizontally.)

```
W I L L G O D T A K E A W A Y M Y F U N D W C B A
L M K P L D B J K W D F D T M T J B P C D H F L W
W H A T I S H E A V E N L I K E D L M F K A T C H
H K D D F S W L D C P J T C M X D L K B M T W P Y
Y F T K M M G T X D P C T B L D L J W C B I K P C
W H A T I S G O D S W I L L P B M F C X W S P L A
O L K P D P P J D C M W T B X K L C Y T P G X K N
N C D O E S G O D R E A L L Y C A R E J W O J F T
T L L Y D K B F F B E T W C Y K X Q Q T X D F C W
G C J B K X W T X F H A B T H Q X J F H K L W X E
O W H Y D O E S G O D A L L O W B A D T H I N G S
D Q T H B W X H Q Z X B T H J Z W X H B X K H Z E
T Z C D D J F W F L V V W Z S S C D B X L E V F E
A S B K D C W F L V X J P S S V F B D C K V P S G
L L D V B C P C L S W W K J P C X R B R W R K S O
K D K P F B W I L L G O D G E T M E I F I M B A D
```

Like the questions hidden in this wordsearch, we frequently hide our questions about God from others. What do you consider the most common reason for doing this?
☐ Asking questions looks like a lack of faith.
☐ We fear God will get mad at us if we ask questions.
☐ We worry that doubts make us bad or weak.
☐ We wonder if we're the only one who asks this question.
☐ Everybody around us seems so certain that we don't want to admit our uncertainties.
☐ _____

If you were to hide a question in the wordsearch puzzle or inside yourself, what question would you hide?

Notice The Value of Honest Questions
Rather than hide your question, go ahead and ask it. Complete Matthew 7:7-8 to discover why you will find the answer:
_____ and it will be _____ to you; _____ and you will _____; _____ and the door will be _____ to you. For everyone who asks _____; he who seeks _____; and to him who knocks, the door will be _____.

Find the courage to ask your questions and explore your doubts by noticing what results come from asking honest questions. Ask yourself:
1. To whom do you go when you need help with a school subject?
2. What do you do when your car breaks down?
3. How do you feel when someone asks you for help with a problem?
4. How might the three answers we've given relate to the way we should ask God questions?

Honest questions are a sign of maturing faith, not faith-lessness. Questions show you trust God to answer you, that you want a religion that works, and that you want a God you can depend on in any circumstance. Dishonest questions do the opposite. How would the following kinds of dishonest questions distance us from God rather than draw us closer to Him?

_____ A question I'm not willing to take the time to answer

_____ A question that excuses me from doing what God asks

_____ A question I ask to cover up what's really bothering me or to distract me from sin in my life

Give an example of a dishonest or insincere question (Example: "Can God make a rock so big He can't move it?")

Are your questions and doubts honest ones? If you're willing to find the answer and live the answer you find, your questions are a sign of faith.

Why could your questions lead to a deeper faith?

(Example: You wonder why bad things happen to good people. You discover in the Bible that God gives the good things, not the bad. You notice that bad things happen to both good and bad people. You no longer have to be mad at God for something He didn't do. You now have freedom to invite God's help for coping with the bad event.)

LIFELINE

Examine the Evidence for God

Before we ask God questions and find His answers, we must first discover that He is really there. We can't find God with scientific experiments or with telescopes, but the evidence for His presence is just as convincing. It's the same kind of evidence that proves friendship or marriage commitment—past and present dependability, communication, consistency, loyalty, helpfulness, guidance, and generosity. In Romans 1:19-20, the same word completes all blanks and tells us who and what reveals God:

Since what may be known about _____ is plain to them, because _____ has made it plain to them. For since the creation of the world _____ 's invisible qualities—His eternal power and divine nature—have been clearly seen, being understood from what has been made, so that men are without excuse.

Consider the following evidence and ask yourself how it points to the reality of God.

NATURE: Nature is not random. It is orderly, consistent, and beautiful. Could this order have happened without a designer to plan it? Could this beauty have happened without a personal, caring creator?

HUMAN INDIVIDUALITY: All human faces have two eyes, a nose, and a mouth, but each one is unique. Why aren't we all clones?

A SENSE OF RIGHT AND WRONG: Even a serial murderer will admit that it's wrong to kill. It's just that he ignored his conscience and acted on his own sinful desires.

THE PRESENCE OF LOVE: How do you explain the fact that human beings care about each other? Why do babies need their parents?

YEARNING FOR SOMETHING MORE: It's not enough to just get up, go to school, do our chores, eat, earn money, and sleep. We want more. We want meaning, relationships, purpose. Where does this yearning come from?

JESUS CHRIST: Jesus is God's ultimate revelation of Himself. Through Jesus, God showed us what He is like. Jesus was also raised from death, never to die again. What else is unique about this man?

THE BIBLE: The Bible describes God and what He is like. It has more evidence for its reliability than other printed documents. What does the Bible say about God's existence?

Find Answers to the Tough Questions
God has revealed Himself, and we can know Him. We don't have to just believe without thinking. God has given us clear evidence for His existence, and we can proudly stake our lives on these facts. How might you answer these

arguments against God? (Most of these arguments can be answered using the evidence we just covered.) Why is the evidence for God stronger than evidence against Him?

"What about hurricanes, tornadoes, and earthquakes? They aren't orderly or beautiful. A good God wouldn't include those in His creation."

"But apes and other higher vertebrates also have unique personalities and do unique things. Perhaps individuality is part of evolution."

"If God cares, why does He make some people more capable or beautiful than others? If God is concerned for us personally, why are there people with handicaps?"

"Some cultures do terrible things like abandon crippled babies or value boy babies above girl babies. They don't seem to understand right and wrong."

"But many people hate and use others. Why would God allow this?"

"Many people seem content with a 9 to 5 routine and don't think past it. They have no room for God in their lives."

"How do we know Christians didn't just make up the Bible?"

IMPORTANT: The real God does not fear being questioned. Steer clear of any religious leader, group, belief, or practice that allows no questions. Fear of questions shows the leader or religion has something to hide. You can ask God anything. The true God, true beliefs, and true practice will stand up under questioning. Ask yourself: Why is it dangerous to believe in God without evidence? How does the evidence for Christianity lead to deeper faith?

 BODYLIFE

Know the Answers Are There

Legitimate questions and doubts have answers. The answers may not be fully comprehensible to us in this lifetime, but answers are there. Because God reveals Himself to us (recall Romans 1:20), we can know Him assuredly and definitely. Tie together what you've explored in this session by doodling or drawing a response to these questions:

How can I know that God is real?

When are doubts.and questions good rather than bad?

Life Response

Commit to know God as He really is and to live your life in that light. Do this with the following covenant or with one you compose. Invite members of the group to witness your covenant. As witnesses, they will sign your covenant, help you seek and find answers, and pray with you as you seek.

I'll Get to K.N.O.W. God

Knowledge — I'll ask my questions and voice my doubts to know God better. As I gain knowledge of God, I'll share my understanding with this group. I'll grow through listening to your insights.
New life — As I know and understand God, I'll show my knowledge and understanding in my actions, attitudes, and words. I'll notice as you do this and will point out what I see God doing through you.
Open to new insights — I won't be afraid of new ideas, because they may be true. I'll listen before I evaluate what you say. Thanks for listening to me.
Without accepting falsehood — I don't want to be so open-minded I crowd out the truth. I'll compare everything I learn to Scripture to verify its truth. I'll then live the truth I discover.

(My Signature)

(Signatures of Group Members)

What's Next?
God may be there, but does He care? What makes you worry that God doesn't care? How does God show His care for you? How do you know God cares about you?

▼

Do You Care about Me, God?

 HEARTBEAT

Why I Want to Know God

Now that we know God is there, we must find out what He is like. Why do you consider this important?

☐ I'm created in God's image. Knowing God helps me know myself and other people better.

☐ I want to know what God is really like, not just what people say He is like.

☐ If I know God, I'll recognize His actions. Then I'll be able to thank Him for what He does, and I won't blame Him for something He didn't do.

☐ Knowing God helps me know what it means to follow Him.

☐ Knowing God shows me how to follow Him.

☐ God is a friend, and I like to get to know my friends.

☐ God created me and can show me how to find and give happiness. As I get to know Him, He can better guide me.

☐ I want to know how to worship God.

☐ Knowing God helps me become more of who He wants me to be and more of who I'm capable of being.

What God Is Like

Draw, doodle, or describe what you think God is like:

As you listen to other group members describe God, record their insights. God is . . .

- •
- •
- •

- •
- •
- •

Though God can never be limited to a human description, how does this exercise help you understand and relate to God? How can you know if your images describe the real God or are hearsay?

 LIFELINE

How God Has Revealed Himself to Us

The Bible is our primary source of specific information about God. Other evidence offers general information about His existence, but it cannot substitute for His Word. Review last week's session by matching what each teaches us about God:

_____ NATURE — a. Shows us that God is love, creates love, and teaches how to love.

_____ HUMAN INDIVIDUALITY — b. Shows us that God cares personally by making each person unique and special.

_____ SENSE OF RIGHT & WRONG — c. Shows that God wants to be with us and wants us to know Him personally.

_____ PRESENCE OF LOVE

_____ YEARNING FOR MORE

_____ JESUS CHRIST

d. Shows us that God is moral and wants right to win out.

e. Shows us that God works in orderly, consistent, and beautiful ways.

f. Shows us that God is spiritual, that there is more to life than what we can see, hear, and touch.

What the Bible Says about God

God gives us many pictures of Himself through the Bible. These pictures help us understand the indescribable God. Unlike the images we composed earlier, these ideas come directly from God. They help us find out how true our images are. Using the Bible passages and illustrations, describe each image in your own words. Then write how you have experienced this characteristic of God or would like to experience it. Place a check mark beside the statement that makes God's character most clear to you and jot down why:

1. God is like a _____. (Psalm 91:4; Matthew 23:37)
I experience this characteristic of God when I . . .

2. God is like an _____. (Exodus 19:4; Isaiah 40:31)
I experience this characteristic of God when I . . .

3. God is like a _____. (Matthew 7:25)
I experience this characteristic of God when I . . .

4. God is like _____. (1 John 1:5; John 1:4-9)
I experience this characteristic of God when I . . .

5. God is like a _____. (Psalms 32:7; 121:7-8)
I experience this characteristic of God when I . . .

6. God is like a _____. (Proverbs 3:5-6; John 14:6)
I experience this characteristic of God when I . . .

7. God is like a _____. (Psalm 139:23-24; John 3:2)
I experience this characteristic of God when I . . .

8. God is like (can be more than one word) _____.
(John 11:25)
I experience this characteristic of God when I . . .

9. God is like a _____. (Psalm 119:45; John 8:36;
Romans 8:2)
I experience this characteristic of God when I . . .

10. God is like a _____. (Psalm 130:3-4; 1 John 1:9)
I experience this characteristic of God when I . . .

11. God is like ——————. (Isaiah 9:6; Matthew 6:9)
I experience this characteristic of God when I . . .

12. God is like ——————. (Isaiah 49:15; 66:13)
I experience this characteristic of God when I . . .

What other image of God have you seen in the Bible?
God is like ——————————————————— .
Bible verse: ——————————————————
I experience this characteristic of God when I . . .

What Believers Say about God
Students of the Bible and followers of God have come up with classic "omni" words (meaning all or completely) to describe God. Three are:

OMNISCIENT means all-knowing. I like this about God because . . .

OMNIPRESENT means present in all places at all times. I like this about God because . . .

OMNIPOTENT means all-powerful. I like this about God because . . .

Think about your favorite Bible verses. What other "all-" words do you see in the Bible? Here are three samples. Fill in others as a group:

All . . .	Bible Passage
All-loving	1 John 4:16
All-seeing	Proverbs 15:3
All-wise	Proverbs 3:1-6
All-_____	
All-_____	

God wants to get up close and personal with you. He has revealed Himself in the Bible and in another very important way. Can you name the most personal way God has revealed Himself? _____

The person Jesus Christ revealed God most personally. He is God Himself in human form. Read His story in the Bible books Matthew, Mark, Luke, or John. Circle the one you will read.

As you read the Bible to learn from it and to understand Jesus, do so in small snatches and do so regularly. This is much easier and more effective than trying to read and digest massive passages at once. Watch for promises of God's love, care, and guidance. Notice how He has revealed Himself in Jesus. As you find promises or characteristics of God, keep a running list in the back of your Bible. Some people write on the inside cover of their Bibles. Others prefer to keep a piece of paper in their Bibles.

 BODYLIFE
The Response God Invites
The God who is really there really cares. His care invites our response. Deuteronomy 30:19-20 summarizes this

18

choice. Read the verse in your Bible to complete these blanks:

This day I call heaven and earth as witnesses against you that I have set before you _____ *and* _____, _____ *and* _____. *Now choose* _____, *so that you and your children may live and that you may* _____ *the Lord your God,* _____ *to His voice, and* _____ _____ *to Him. For the Lord is your* _____, *and He will give you many years in the land He swore to give to your fathers, Abraham, Isaac and Jacob (Deuteronomy 30:19-20).*

Deuteronomy 30:11-14 reminds us that we can make a choice for God and keep it. Read it in your Bible to discover that responding to God is not _____ or _____ your reach. It is not up in _____ or across the _____. God and His Word are very close. We make contact simply by talking to Him. We accept His love in the midst of our imperfections and respond by loving Him back.

Deuteronomy 6:4-5 summarizes how to live out a choice for God. Use your Bible to find these actions that show your response to God:
Hear, O Israel: The Lord our God, the Lord is one. _____ *the Lord your God with all your* _____ *and with all your* _____ *and with all your* _____.

Christians call a decision for God "salvation." We recognize that we aren't good enough to approach the Almighty God, but He has bridged this gap by coming in the person of Jesus Christ. The Book of Romans describes what it means to be saved. Romans 10:9-11 explains that salvation is both an event and a relationship. Romans 12:1-2 describes the continual commitment that shows when a Christian walks closely with God. Underline these verses in your Bible. Circle words you consider most important.

19

We'll study specific ways to relate to the real God in upcoming sessions of this study. But right now, write what you think relating to the real God means in the light of Romans 10:9-10; 12:1-2 and Deuteronomy 6:4-5; 30:11-20:

Do you want life in all its fullness and adventure? Then grow a personal relationship with God. Knowing God begins with recognizing Him and continues with trusting Him to care for you. Let Him know you, cleanse you, guide you. Express your trust by obeying Him. Hebrews 11:6 calls this faith. Circle the word in your Bible. Then describe faith by completing these statements:

Faith in God means . . .

God wants us to show commitment to Him by . . .

You can tell a person believes in God when . . .

Life Response
Check the box that most closely describes your faith in God up to this point. Feel free to describe your commitment on the blank line.

☐ I believe He is there, but I haven't let Him affect my life.

☐ I have made a personal commitment to God but have made no connection between God and my daily life.

☐ I call on God mainly when the going gets rough.

DO YOU CARE ABOUT ME, GOD?

☐ I go to church frequently but on other days I'm just like anybody else.

☐ I know that God cares about my daily life, so God and I talk and walk together through each event.

☐ I show my faith in God by thanking Him, listening to Him, obeying Him.

☐ _____

Now check or write the faith commitment(s) you want to make from this day forward:

☐ I will communicate with God daily so I can understand what to do, when to do it, how to do it.

☐ I will draw on God's strength in both good times and bad, so I can obey Him consistently.

☐ I will make every day a day of worship by choosing actions, thoughts, words, and activities that bring glory to God. I recognize that doing well and acting kindly at school, work, and home bring honor to God.

☐ I will learn to love like God loves and express this love with all my heart, soul, and strength.

☐ I will take God seriously and get to know Him so I can decide whether or not to commit to Him.

☐ _____

God's existence means little if He's just an impersonal force. Let Him make a difference in your life. Circle the synonym for God that you most want and need right now:

Lord	Savior	Master	Friend
Adviser	Forgiver	Freedom	Teacher

What's Next?

Where is God when the going gets rough? Name something many people believe about God in tough times that is not true. Then think about something many people believe about God in tough times that *is* true.

▼

THREE

Will You Get Me If I'm Bad, God?

 HEARTBEAT

When the Going Gets Rough

How does your relationship with God change when things go wrong? When something sad happens, relating to God can be tough or easy, depending on how you see Him. Look around the room or in your purse or wallet for an item that shows how you see God when things go wrong. Complete these sentences using that item as a teaching tool:

When things go wrong, God is like ———— because . . .

But He is different from ———————— because . . .

Lean on God

What we believe about God determines how we relate to Him. Some of the following beliefs about God are true, some are false, and some are partly true. Write in your books a reason you agree or a reason you disagree with each statement:

God throws lightning bolts or blessings at you, depending on how you act.
I agree because. . . .   I disagree because. . . .

God punishes people who do wrong.
I agree because. . . .   I disagree because. . . .

When something bad happens, it means God is angry.
I agree because. . . .   I disagree because. . . .

When bad things happen, it means God didn't care enough to stop it.
I agree because. . . .   I disagree because. . . .

Everything that happens is God's will.
I agree because. . . .   I disagree because. . . .

God responds to wrong by giving good.
I agree because. . . .   I disagree because. . . .

God allows the wrong for our growth.
I agree because. . . .   I disagree because. . . .

 LIFELINE

See God As He Really Is

Mistaken images of God can make us turn away from God, fear Him, or fight against Him. True images bring us close to God, empower us, and give us security. We've got to notice the way God really is, rather than just believe what we've heard. What reasons does Psalm 119 give for getting to know the real God? Focus on verses 9-11, 18, 28, 41-42, 76, 98, 133.

What caution does Job 42:7 offer about what we believe and teach about God?

Our beliefs determine how we relate to God and to other people. How would believing these statements impact how we relate to God? To people?

If I believe God is out to get me, I will . . .

If I believe God wants to take away my fun, I will . . .

If I believe God is responsible for the bad things in my life, I will . . .

If I believe God genuinely cares about me, I will . . .

If I believe God gives the good and Satan or people give the bad, I will . . .

If I believe God wants to let me in on the inside scoop on life, I will . . .

Discover the Joy of Obedience

Relating to God during bad times does not have to be different from relating to Him during good times: We can continue to find ways to please God and obey Him because we love Him. God gives us power to do this. First Peter 4:12, 19 summarizes this idea. Unscramble the key words:

Dear friends, do not be EIDUPRRSS at the painful trial you are experiencing, as though something AEGNRST were happening to you . . . those who suffer . . . should TCIOMM themselves to their AFFIUHLT Creator and continue to do OGDO.

How has committing to your faithful Creator helped you through hard times?

What good do you continue to do during hard times? (For instance, do you keep patient even when you feel like lashing out? Do you think of others' feelings besides your own?)

How does obedience bring freedom rather than confinement?

Read Psalm 51:10-12. How does obedience bring joy?

Job is remembered today for his patience. In truth, however, his strongest characteristics were faithfulness to God and an insistence on answers (Job 13:15-16). The Prophet Habakkuk knew that the answers would certainly come, even if they were slow in coming (Habakkuk 2:3). What enables you, or would enable you, to trust God and do good when things go wrong?

IMPORTANT: When sad things happen, you may not feel God's care. This doesn't mean God has left you; it means you are numb with pain. God is not a feeling but a Steady Presence who never leaves you (see Romans 8:38-39). God goes with you through the worst trials and the brightest joys. He is he constant in your life. Psalm 23 presents a vivid picture of God's care. Write this psalm in your own words:

 BODYLIFE

Keep Wrestling with Hard Questions

Even when we understand the basics, we still wrestle with questions about pain. That's OK. Keep wrestling while you trust, and keep trusting while you wrestle. Practice with these questions:

When things go wrong, some people get mad at God. They think He's mad at them or out to get them. Or they think He should protect them from the sad and tragic events of life. What does the Bible and your experience with God say about these ideas?

Why do you think some people wonder about God only when things go bad? Why don't they eagerly embrace God when things go well?

Life Response

Honest wrestling with real-life questions is tough. But too often when friends (even ourselves) go through hard times, we give a pat answer expecting that answer to clear up the pain. Real-life healing is not that instant. Let's be loving representatives of Christ, not answer-spouting comforters of Job (recall the warning in Job 42:7). Respond to each case study, then anonymously trade books and give each other a "pat rating."

CASE STUDY 1: I was born with a disease called cystic fibrosis. Unless a cure is found, the disease may eventually kill me. I'm glad I was born, and I'm glad I'm me, but I wish I didn't have this disease. I'm a Christian and try to do right, but the disease remains. I don't understand why God won't cure me, or even why there's cystic fibrosis at all.

THE WAY I'D RESPOND:

PAT RATING FROM THE GROUP FOR MY RESPONSE:

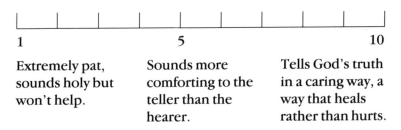

1	5	10
Extremely pat, sounds holy but won't help.	Sounds more comforting to the teller than the hearer.	Tells God's truth in a caring way, a way that heals rather than hurts.

CASE STUDY 2: Last year, a gas explosion destroyed our house and almost killed my brother. We didn't know there was a gas leak, and when my brother entered the house and turned on the stove, the house exploded. He spent months in the hospital and has horrible scars. If God really cared, He wouldn't have let this happen to us. It's not fair.

THE WAY I'D RESPOND:

PAT RATING FROM THE GROUP FOR MY RESPONSE:

1	5	10
Extremely pat, sounds holy but won't help.	Sounds more comforting to the teller than the hearer.	Tells God's truth in a caring way, a way that heals rather than hurts.

What's Next?
How does faith in God differ from religion? How do you show you have real faith?

▼

How Do I Believe in You, God?

 HEARTBEAT
Can You See My Faith?

Once we believe God is there, commit ourselves to knowing Him, and discard false images of Him, we are ready to live our faith every day. At the same time, living our faith in daily life helps us recognize that God is there, makes us want to commit ourselves more firmly to Him, and helps us recognize true and false images. Belief and practice work hand in hand. In this session, we'll explore how to express our faith.

Choose your favorite response to the following statement or write your own. Then jot in your book why you chose the answer you did.

1. Faith in God is . . .
   a. something you have.
   b. something you do.
   c. trusting God enough to obey Him.
   d. a relationship.
   e. _____

2. My faith in God grows . . .
   a. when I obey God and see how wise He really is.
   b. when I watch the results of Christlike actions.
   c. when I see other Christians express their faith.
   d. as I get to know God better.
   e. _____

3. You can tell if people believe in God by . . .
   a. watching the way they treat people.
   b. watching how they handle problems.
   c. listening to the way they talk.
   d. noticing their lifestyle, what they do and don't do.
   e. _____

4. I show I believe in God by . . .
   a. valuing what He values: people, feelings, right behavior and attitudes, genuineness, honesty.
   b. obeying Him in everyday life.
   c. leaning on Him in rough times and rejoicing with Him in good.
   d. rejecting counterfeit happiness—happiness based on money, popularity, and status.
   e. _____

5. I think the most important element of faith is . . .
   a. trust.
   b. consistency.
   c. relationship.
   d. communication.
   e. obedience.
   f. _____

 LIFELINE

Faith Is Something You Do

How can you show you believe in God, that you have a life changing relationship with Him? James 1:22–2:25 explains that actions are evidence of the faith we have. Fill in the blanks by comparing these excerpts with your Bible:

1:22: *Do not merely _____ to the word, and so _____ yourselves. _____ what it says.*

2:14: *What good is it my brothers, if a man claims to have _____ but has no _____. Can such a faith save him?*

2:18: *But someone will say, "You have _____; I have _____." Show me your _____ without _____, and I will show you my _____ by what I _____.*

2:22: *You see that his _____ and his _____ were working together, and his faith was made complete by what he _____.*

2:26: *As the body without the _____ is dead, so _____ without _____ is dead.*

Read James 2:14-26 to complete these examples of faith:
1. If a sister or brother . . .

2. Our ancestor Abraham was considered righteous for . . .

3. Rahab the prostitute was considered righteous for . . .

Can you think of a way to show faith without actions?

According to James 2:19, who or what believes in God but doesn't have faith?

Faith, also called belief, is something you show in your actions. You don't possess it like a merit badge—you live it. Habakkuk 2:4 explains: *The righteous shall live by his faith.* The Hebrew term translated "faith" in this verse can also be translated "faithfulness." Faith is something you do; it's action and attitude.

To show righteousness is to do right based on a loving relationship with God. Describe a way to show righteousness through faithfulness.

Faith Must Come from the Heart

Christian actions don't make us Christians any more than hanging apples on a tree would make the tree an apple tree. The fruit must come from what's on the inside. First we accept God through Jesus Christ. Then our actions become a tribute to our love for God. First Corinthians 13:1, 3 says it this way: *If I speak in the tongues of men and of angels, but have not love, I am only a resounding gong or a clanging cymbal . . . If I give all I possess to the poor and surrender my body to the flames, but have not love, I gain nothing.*

Many people go through the motions of faithfulness without heart obedience, without true loyalty. This absence of loyalty is like dating someone who doesn't seem to care. You can tell she or he's not interested in you, but he or she goes through the motions. When questioned, he or she says, "But what am I not DOing?" Jesus called such people hypocrites. Use your Bible to complete Jesus' description in Matthew

23:27-28: *"Woe to you, teachers of the law and Pharisees, you _____! You are like whitewashed _____, which look _____ on the outside but on the inside are full of _____ men's _____ and everything unclean. In the same way, on the _____ you appear to people as _____ but on the inside you are full of hypocrisy and wickedness."*

Hypocrites make me feel . . .

I'm a hypocrite when . . .

I think God's prescription for hypocrisy is . . .

I Can Be Faithful

The good news is that you don't have to stay hypocritical, and you don't have to settle for mediocre faithfulness. You can make choices that lead to an exciting life with God. Many call this a "walk with Christ." To find this adventure, obey God in each decision and action. Find out how to obey God by reading the Bible. Read a paragraph or two every day and do what it tells you to do.

Second, notice why God's ways work. Observe how His guidelines bring happiness to you and those around you. Practice by naming reasons these ten rules of God work. They are known as the Ten Commandments, and you can find them in Exodus 20:1-17. The last one is done as an example of what a student might write.

ARE YOU THERE, GOD?

Command	Pain Caused by Disobeying	Happiness Brought by Obeying
1. You shall have no other gods besides me.		
2. You shall not make for yourself an idol.		
3. You shall not misuse the name of the Lord your God.		
4. Remember the Sabbath Day. Six days you shall labor and do all your work, but on the seventh day you shall not do any work.		
5. Honor your father and your mother.		
6. You shall not murder.		
7. You shall not commit adultery.		
8. You shall not steal.		
9. You shall not give false testimony against your neighbor.		
10. You shall not covet your neighbor's house, wife, servant, ox, donkey, or anything that belongs to your neighbor.	Coveting would cause pain because I'd resent my neighbor and might compete with her. It would divide our friendship.	Brings happiness because I learn to be happy with what I have. I can also be happy for my neighbor.

Name a way you will specifically live out one of these ten commandments. State it without a "no," "not," or any negative. In other words, name what you will do rather than what you won't:

To obey commandment # _____ I'll

 BODYLIFE

I Obey to Show My Faith

Is all this struggling to show faithfulness worth it? John 10:10 says: *The _____ comes only to steal and kill and destroy; I have come that they may have _____ , and have it to the _____ .*

According to this verse and my experience with God, it is worth it to show my belief in Him because:

Do you want life in all its fullness and adventure or do you prefer a weaker, less fun option that means missing out on at least some happiness?

Not only can God give us life in all its fullness, He also cares. Jeremiah 31:3 is one of the many Bible tributes to God's love for us:

The Lord appeared to us in the past, saying: "I have loved you with an everlasting love; I have drawn you with loving-kindness."

Why is God's love the most important motivation for faithfulness to Him? Why is love stronger than threat of punishment? Draw or describe your answer:

Life Response

Joshua 24:14-15 explains that each of us chooses whether or not we will be faithful to God. Our parents can't do it. Our friends can't do it. God won't do it. You choose to follow Him initially, and you choose to affirm or deny that commitment with every action, decision, and attitude. What will you choose?

Now fear the Lord and serve Him with all faithfulness . . . if serving the Lord seems undesirable to you, then choose for yourselves this day whom you will serve . . . But as for me and my household, we will serve the Lord.

Zeda had been a Christian for three years before she realized God was interested in her everyday life. She felt great about Sundays and church stuff. But her Mondays through Saturdays were lousy. She didn't realize faith and life could and should connect. When she discovered that God could help her make sense out of friendship squabbles and guide her through family pain, Zeda felt as though she'd been set free.

How could God transform Zeda's life? Your life? Reread James 1:22–2:25 and Exodus 20:1-17. Write at least one faithful action and one faithful attitude you'll express to demonstrate the transforming power of God in each of these areas of your life:

FAMILY:

FRIENDSHIP:

SCHOOL:

CHURCH:

FREE TIME:

WHAT I READ:

WHAT I LISTEN TO/THINK ABOUT:

DATING:

PLAYING/WATCHING SPORTS:

MONEY:

TELEVISION:

One final word: Faithfulness is a choice, not a feeling. There are times you'll feel all gushy and happy and confident about your relationship with God. There will be other times when you feel empty and sad. In both times, choose to show faithfulness to God. He will stay faithful to you.

What's Next?
What is the will of God for your life? For today? For this hour?

▼

What Do You Want from Me, God?

 HEARTBEAT

It's No Secret

We often think of God's will as an elusive secret waiting to be discovered. But most of God's will has already been revealed in the Bible. If you have read the Bible, you already know some of God's will. Beginning with each letter (or sound) of the alphabet, name something you know is God's will. Two have been completed for you.

A
B
C
D
E
Faithfulness to God
G
H
I
J
K
L

M
N
O
P
Q
R
S
T
U
V
W
Xtra kind actions when I'm feeling grumpy
Y
Z

These already revealed elements of God's will can help you make difficult major decisions like "Whom will I marry?" and "What career should I choose?" We know, for example, to marry only caring Christians because the Bible instructs us to do so (2 Corinthians 6:14). We know to be honest in our studies because God encourages us to be honest workers (2 Timothy 2:15). We know to choose an occupation that brings glory to God because the Bible says to do all things for God (Colossians 3:23). What the Bible doesn't give is the name of the person to marry, the college or training program to attend, or the specific occupation to choose. We use the principles found in the Bible to deduce answers to our questions. What do the ABC examples of God's will teach you about the big decisions you face right now?

Move beyond the Myths
Too many Christians buy into the myth that God's will is the opposite of their will. To see how incorrect this thinking is, name at least three things you want that God also wants:

1.
2.
3.

Christians can have solid marriages, faithful friendships, a constant sense of purpose, and consistent happiness. These gems of life are a few of the things God wants that we want. But if God wants what we want, why should we seek God's will? Because He and only He knows how to build solid marriages, solidify faithful friendships, and so on. When God's will is different from ours, do as He says. When His will matches our goals, follow His plan for reaching the goal. As we obey God, we find the happiness we seek. We live His will.

Another widely believed myth is that following God's will robs you of all your fun. Name three examples or reasons obeying God frees you rather than binds you:

1.
2.
3.

 LIFELINE

The first key to God's will is found in James 1:22-27. You briefly studied verse 22 in session 4. It is written here in code. To read it, draw lines that separate the words properly:

Don otme rely li stent ot hew ord,a n ds odec e i vey our sel ves.D ow hat its ays.

The second key, in Proverbs 3:1-5, explains that knowing the word is not the same as doing it. We've got to know how to do it. Herein is wisdom. To understand how to do God's will, draw lines that separate the words properly:

Don o tf orge tmy tea chin g,bu tke epmy com man d sin you rhea rt,f orth eyw ill pro lon gyo url i fema nyy ears an dbrin gyo upros perit y.le tlo vean dfa ith fuln essn everl eav ey ou; bin dt hem a roun dyou rne ck,wr itet hemo n thet able to fyo urhe art. The nyo uwil lwin fav oran dag oo dnam ein t hes ig hto fG odan dma n.t rust int heLo rdwi thal lyo urhe arta ndle anno ton yo urow nun ders tan ding; i nally our wa ysack now ledge him,a n dhew illm akey ourp at hss traig ht.

Find God's Will Every Time You Read the Bible

Discover what God has to say by reading the Bible. Read at least a paragraph every day. Each time you read the Bible, you will better understand what God's will is. Then do it.

God's will comes in several forms: commands, guidelines, and balanced actions. You studied ten commands in the last session (review Exodus 20:1-17). Unscramble these eight guidelines, using the Bible passages for clues:

CAT UTJLYS	(Micah 6:6-8)
OVEL ECMYR	(Micah 6:6-8)
AKWL BMUHYL TIHW ORYU OGD	(Micah 6:6-8)
RFOEF UORY EOBDIS SA IIGLVN ARSCFICISE	(Romans 12:1-2)
EB DROTARNFSEM YB HTE NGERENIW FO RYUO IMDN	(Romans 12:1-2)
ETTS NAD OEPARPV TAWH OGD'S IWLL SI	(Romans 12:1-2)
EB FELS EOTCONLRDL NAD TALRE	(1 Peter 5:8)
PSRU NOE RANTOEH ROTAWD EOLV NAD ODOG EESDD	(Hebrews 10:24)

Choose one guideline from the above list and name a way it guides how you act at school, work, or home:

Finally, God's will comes in pairs of balanced actions. Sometimes you find pairs of balancing actions in different verses, sometimes in the same verse. In the following verses, how does each pair of actions work together to produce God's will?

You were called to be *balanced with* Serve one another
free (Gal. 5:13).   in love (Gal. 5:13).

Look to the interests   *balanced with* Do not throw your
of others (Phil. 2:4).   pearls to pigs (Matt. 7:6).

If someone is caught   *balanced with* Watch yourself or you
in a sin, you who are   may also be tempted
spiritual should   (Gal. 6:1).
restore him gently
(Gal. 6:1).

The love of money is *balanced with* If anyone does not
the root of all kinds   provide for his relatives
of evil (1 Tim. 6:10).   and especially his
                                 immediate family, he
                                 has denied the faith
                                 and is worse than
                                 an unbeliever
                                 (1 Tim. 5:8).

How would the above Bible guidelines and balanced actions help you determine answers to these specific questions?

Whom shall I sit with at lunch?

Whom shall I grow a close friendship with?

Whom shall I date?

What should I do with my time?

What skills shall I develop?

Where should I live?

How shall I celebrate?

How shall I handle my problems?

Your current question about God's will:

 **BODYLIFE**

Doing God's will is a day-by-day thing, not something you save for the big decisions of life. Living according to God's will in the daily things prepares you for and makes it easier to recognize God's will in the big things. For example:

FINDING GOD'S WILL FOR YOUR MARRIAGE happens as you. . . .

Step 1	Step 2	Step 3
Notice the value in each person and treat everyone as a person of worth. Keep this in mind as you get to know people.	This draws you to people of genuine worth rather than individuals who crave popularity. It also helps you know the real person rather than an image.	By following the first two steps, you'll be more likely to meet and grow close to someone who will value you like God values you.

Why is this step-by-step seeking of God's will better than waiting until after you're dating someone seriously to ask, "Do You like this one, God?" or "Is this the one You want me to marry?"

What three steps might lead to living God's will in the other big decisions you make? Fill in a step by step chart for other big decisions:

FINDING THE OCCUPATION GOD WANTS for you happens as you . . .

Step 1   Step 2   Step 3

CHOOSING THE COLLEGE/JOB TRAINING God wants for you happens as you . . .

Step 1   Step 2   Step 3

Life Response

God's will is something to get in on, not something to dread or surrender to. Romans 12:1-2 explains that God's will is _____, _____, and _____.

How have you found living God's will to be *good?*

How have you found living God's will to be *pleasing?*

How have you found living God's will to be *perfect?*

Write your name vertically (up and down). Beginning with each letter of your first name, describe a way you'll live God's good, pleasing, and perfect will. Consider such areas as home, school, church, and free time.

What's Next?

How does living in harmony with God produce the happiest, the most fun-loving, and the most exciting life?

▼

Do You Really Make Any Difference, God?

 HEARTBEAT

This Is the Life!

How does God make life worth living? Worth celebrating?

Why is daily life with God happier, deeper, richer, more exciting, and more real than other choices?

How does God give you contentment and security?

With what superlatives (happiest, fullest, richest, etc.) would you describe your life with God?

Advertisements and commercials continually proclaim products and services in superlatives: the best, the most indispensable, the richest, strongest, and so on. If an advertising company wrote a commercial for the Christian life, what would it say? What would you say? Using the perks, benefits, and bests you've jotted above, write a commercial that tells why Christianity is the best life, a life we can't be without.

 LIFELINE

You've named reasons you believe life with God is the greatest. How did you arrive at those reasons? Perhaps by studying and living the Bible, or by watching other people who study and live the Bible. To truly understand and live for God, you must get to know Him as He really is. The way to do this is to study the Bible for yourself. First John 2:27 assures us that God reveals Himself and His purposes to us. With this in mind, let's practice some Bible interpretation skills.

Pick Out the Nuggets

Compare our search for truth to mining. Like miners, we use the light God provides us to find valuable truths in a spiritually darkened world.

Many passages contain lists of truth. Lift them out and examine them. Read Proverbs 2:1-15 to practice nugget mining. What advantages of understanding and living for God do you find there?

Verse 5:	Verse 5:
Verse 7:	Verse 7:
Verse 8:	Verse 8:
Verse 9:	Verse 9:
Verse 10:	
Verse 11:	Verse 11:
Verses 12-15:	

Spend the Wealth

These nuggets won't do you much good if you don't cash them in and spend them in your life. After you find the truth, ponder how to apply it to your own life. Complete these sentences to help you apply Proverbs 2:1-15.

Understanding the fear of the Lord (v. 5) does not mean I'll be afraid of God, but that I'll . . .

God's provision of victory (v. 7) doesn't mean I'll win every contest I enter, but that . . .

God's protection (vv. 8, 11) doesn't mean I can do anything I want to do and not be hurt, but that . . .

Understanding every good path (v. 9) doesn't mean the answers I find will be easy. It means . . .

Being saved from wicked people (vv. 12-15) urges me to avoid involvement with wicked people because . . .

Mine the Truth

Many Bible passages have themes or pervasive truths that run throughout them. Sometimes you have to dig around, read and reread, before you notice them. Wisdom is the theme that flows through Proverbs 2:1-15. Wisdom can be defined as *applying real truth to real life.* Name someone you know who is wise: _____. Using both Proverbs 2:1-15 and your experience, describe how this person demonstrates his or her wisdom:

How will you imitate both this person's example and Proverbs 2:1-15 to exhibit wisdom in your life?

Wear Safety Equipment

Life on earth is full of dangers. Though Christianity doesn't guarantee a trouble-free existence, obedience to God helps us avoid most of the dangers. If you show kindness to friends, they tend to be much more loyal to you. If you save sexual intimacy for marriage, feelings of marital loyalty and oneness tend to be stronger. If you point out the good in people, they tend to live out that good.

In His Sermon on the Mount (Matthew 5–7), Jesus tells His listeners of "safety equipment" that can help them avoid sin and live closer to God. For each of the following dangers in life, name a safety action from chapter 7 that could have prevented the trouble. Then suggest an alternate action plan:

1. In her desire to make friends, Celina began loaning money. Instead of returning the money, her new "friends"

just kept asking for more. When she quit loaning, they spread an ugly rumor about her.

Safety Action from Chapter 7:

Alternate Plan:

2. Andy doesn't remember what started the questions. He only knows that when he started asking how people know God is real, they just told him to quit doubting and believe. He wants answers, but no one gives them. He decides to give up on Christianity.

Safety Action from Chapter 7:

Alternate Plan:

3. After they dated for six months Amanda and her boyfriend began having sex. She knew it was wrong, but it seemed so right. Because so many people at her school had sex, it didn't seem so bad. She used birth control, and they practiced safe sex. But Amanda had trouble sleeping at night. The joy she and her boyfriend had shared seemed to fade away.

Safety Action from Chapter 7:

Alternate Plan:

4. Carl decided he'd go to church and invest in spiritual things when he got older. He had too many other commit-

ments right now. He needed a football scholarship so he practiced football every spare minute. But an injury in his senior year ended his promising career. He had neither the grades nor the relationship with God to handle his predicament.

Safety Action from Chapter 7:

Alternate Plan:

What other trouble might principles in Matthew 7 prevent?

Choose the Happy Path

Much happiness and security depends on choosing the right path in the first place. Second Corinthians 6:14 suggests a way of ensuring good, close relationships. Rephrase this verse using positive words. (In other words, instead of emphasizing the problems of relationships with unbelievers, write about the benefits of close relationships with believers.)

How does choosing friends and dates who have much in common with you, including confidence in God, help your whole life go more smoothly?

Notice Why It's Right

Perhaps the most important Bible skill is learning to agree with God. "Why?" "How?" and "Is it worth it?" are important questions that have real answers. Every time you read the Bible, notice why God's ways work in real life. Remember that God came to earth and lived by His rules. As we recognize God's wisdom and decide to obey Him, we find the happy life we seek. How would the actions in Romans 12:9-21 help you when . . .

there's an argument going on?

somebody's not being straight with you?

you're tired and cross?

something unfair has happened?

everything's going great?

you want to go out with somebody who doesn't seem to notice you?

What is your most recent trauma? How could God help you with it?

 BODYLIFE

The main way to discover how life with God makes a difference is to live it. Living for God is not talking in a holy sounding voice, going to church all the time, or walking around with your head in the clouds. It's obeying God in everyday life. It's getting in touch with what really matters. This might mean something as simple as inviting a lonely friend to sit at your table. It may be as complex as giving up your habit of lying, so you can glorify God in your home life.

Describe a time you applied the Bible to your life and discovered a happier, more fulfilling way:

What do you think God wants you to start doing (or stop doing) so that you can live the good life?

Living the good life is also a group thing. How has our group cooperated with God to create belonging, answers, purpose, love?

Life Response
God not only exists; He gives you personal care, steady love, and trustworthy guidance. Titus 3:8 summarizes why God's ways bring the best life in the universe. Unscramble the scrambled words to discover why:
This is a trustworthy saying. And I want you to stress these things, so that those who have trusted in God may be careful to devote themselves to doing what is good. These things are — EEECLLNTX and ABEFOILPRT for EEENORVY.

Write a covenant between yourself and God to live your life for Him; then take the actions that will ensure that lifestyle. Let these sentences get you started, but don't end there:

Because God made me and the rest of creation, He is the one who is best qualified to guide me to the good life. My life will show I trust Him when I . . .

Because God is God, He can guide me to build the strongest friendships, the closest marriage, the most meaningful work. To do this, I will . . .

The good life doesn't consist of fame, wealth, and power, but of good things that can't fade away. I want my life to include qualities like (circle your choices):

Strong friendships	Patience
Integrity	Success measured by do-
Genuineness	ing my best
True love	Kindness
Sensitivity	Trust
A family that really cares	Compassion
about each other	Understanding
Wisdom	Confidence
Peace	Joy

What's Next?

Recall each lesson you've learned in this study. Live your life in touch with the God who is there, who cares personally for you, who communicates what He is really like, who can guide your daily life, who shows you what to do, and who is the Author of the good life.

Other SonPower Small Group Studies that can guide you as you get to know and live for God include *What's a Kid Like Me Doing in a Family Like This?* (on family relationships) and *Can't Fight the Feelings* (on emotions).

Are You There, God?

Please take a minute to fill out and mail this form giving us your candid reaction to this material. Thanks for your help!

Did you enjoy this book? Why or why not?

How has this book helped you . . .
- grow closer to your group?

- grow closer to God?

Would you like to use other SonPower Small Group Studies?

In what setting did you use this book? (circle one)

Sunday School   youth group   midweek Bible study

Other:_____

How many members were in your group?

What grade are you in?

(OPTIONAL)
         Name   _____

         Address _____

SonPower Youth Sources Editor
Victor Books
1825 College Avenue
Wheaton, Illinois 60187